D0767673

Computer
Games Designer

Mark Featherstone

Raintree is an imprint of Capstone Global Library Limited, a company incorporated in England and Wales having its registered office at 7 Pilgrim Street, London, EC4V 6LB – Registered company number: 6695582

www.raintreepublishers.co.uk
myorders@raintreepublishers.co.uk

Text © Capstone Global Library Limited 2014
First published in hardback in 2014
Paperback imprint published in 2015
The moral rights of the proprietor have been asserted.

Edited by Nancy Dickmann, Adam Miller, Laura Knowles, and Helen Cox Cannons
Designed by Richard Parker, and Emily Hooton at Ken Bell Graohic Design
Picture research by Mica Brancic
Originated by Capstone Global Library Ltd.
Production by Vicki Fitzgerald
Printed and bound in China by CTPS

ISBN 978 1 406 25979 7 (hardback)
17 16 15 14 13
10 9 8 7 6 5 4 3 2 1

ISBN 978 1 406 25984 1 (paperback)
18 17 16 15 14
10 9 8 7 6 5 4 3 2 1

British Library Cataloguing in Publication Data
Featherstone, Mark.
   Computer games designer. -- (The coolest jobs on the planet)
   1. Computer games--Design--Juvenile literature.
   2. Computer games--Design--Vocational guidance--Juvenile
   literature.
   I. Title II. Series
   794.8'1526-dc23

Acknowledgements
We would like to thank the following for permission to reproduce photographs: Alamy pp. 11 (© betty finney), 15 (© David J. Green – technology), 35 (© Silicon Valley Stock); © David Braben and Ian Bell p.14; © Capstone Global Library Ltd p. 18 (Steve Mead); Arkham Horror is ™ Fantasy Flight Games p. 39; CCP Games p. 28; Corbis p. 19 (© Mark Savage); Getty Images pp. 9 (Photographer's Choice/Seth Joel), 22 (Ethan Miller), 25 (Bloomberg/Chris Ratcliffe), 27 (EA/Jeff Vinnick), 32 (AFP Photo/Joe Klamar), 33 (WireImage/Albert L. Ortega), 37 (Stone+/Nick Dolding); Mark Featherstone pp. 4, 8, 20, 21, 26 inset, 26 main, 29, 40; Metacritic p. 5; Microsoft p. 30; Photoshot p. 31 (Richard B Levine); Planetside Software pp. 24 l & r; Rex Features pp. 6 (Camilla Morandi), 7 (Graham Harrison), 10 (Andy Drysdale), 12 (Terry Harris), 13 (Future Publishing/Gavin Roberts), 23 (James Curley); Sheffield Hallam University p.16; Shutterstock p.34 (© Yaroslavna); Sumo Digital p.36; Valve Corporation p.38.

Background design images supplied by Shutterstock (© AND Inc, © Archipoch, © Athanasia Nomikou, © donatas1205, © dundanim, © fotographic1980, © Ghenadie, © hfng, © isak55, © Kotkoa, © Lonely, © Lukas Radavicius, © Manczurov, © Michelangelus, © Olga Miltsova, © Petr Vaclavek, © Phunya, © Sasha Chebotarev, © Serg Obolonkov, © Skocko, © Tjeffersion, © watchara, © zirconicusso).

Cover pictures of a Sci-fi city, a futuristic soldier, and a matrix-wireframe reproduced with permission of Shutterstock (© AND Inc., © DarkGeometryStudios, © Archipoch).

CONTENTS

The moment of truth

The most exciting moments in game development are when the game you've worked on for so many months – or even years – is finally ready. Playing the completed game for the first time, it feels almost magical as you see all your ideas brought to life. Then comes certification, when your publisher checks what you've done and decides if they think the game is ready for the public. Shortly after that is the launch day, and you visit the local games shop and buy one of the first copies of the finished game. The publisher will give you a free copy, but it isn't the same as buying one from the shop!

This is one of my games still in its shiny wrapper, never to be opened!

XBOX

PAL

GUNMETAL

Rage

> I always check a website called Metacritic, which summarizes reviews of computer games. If one of my games gets a positive score then I know I've done well!

Reviews

The next big moment comes when the first reviews come in. Some are by professional critics, but many more are by members of the public posting on websites. If people have enjoyed playing your game, and say nice things, it feels wonderful. Sometimes the comments aren't all nice, but at least you can learn something and make the next game a little bit better.

Did you know?

Reviews are really important. Some game developers get paid a bonus depending on how well their game scores on Metacritic, which collects all the different review scores together into one average score.

The process of making a game

Let's back up a little. Launch day is incredibly exciting, but a lot of work has to happen before then:

1. The idea – everyone contributes ideas, especially the publisher.
2. The pitch – we present an idea to managers and publishers.
3. Prototyping – we need exciting new game play and visuals. Small programs are made to demonstrate them.
4. Pre-production – all the tools needed are programmed. Staff are hired and trained.
5. Alpha – tools are ready, so it's time to make the 3D models, and build the levels. No new features allowed after this stage!
6. Beta – everything is finished, but it doesn't play quite right and crashes constantly! Get it fixed! (I'm pretty sure no game ever worked perfectly the first time.)
7. Certification – the publisher's testers check everything. They don't work with us, so there's no chance of bias.
8. Release – time for a party before we start again! Check the reviews.

MY HERO!
TETSUYA NOMURA
(BORN 1970)

Tetsuya Nomura is one of the artists at SquareEnix, makers of the *Final Fantasy* role playing games. He's absolutely brilliant.

What does a games programmer do?

Programming is all about breaking everything down into smaller and more easily understandable parts. A program is like a machine: it's built out of many different inter-locking pieces. When you look at the whole problem, you cannot even begin to understand how you might tackle it, but if you look at just one small piece then it becomes easier.

An old game such as *Space Invaders* (one of my childhood favourites) looks simple now. But even games like this took a team of programmers a long time to put together!

Even Richard Branson loved *Space Invaders!*

A day in the life

I'm an independent developer, which means I'm my own boss. Here's what an average day is like:

8.30–10.00 am	Take my daughter to school, walk my dog, and think about the game
10.00–10.30	Talk to the team – what's next? Add any new bugs to the bug list.
10.30–11.00	Generate publicity for the game
11.00–12.00	Programming work based on the bugs list
12.00–1.00 pm	Lunch
1.00–3.00	Check the design; start programming the next task
3.00–4.00	Pick my daughter up
4.00–5.30	Play the new game and test everything is working
5.30–6.00	Admin, taxes, and paperwork
6.00–9.00	Family time
9.00–11.30	More programming!

Here I am hard at work on a game.

Working for a big developer

In the past, I worked for big developers. My day was very different then as I wasn't running the business – I could concentrate on programming.

8.30–10.00 am	Discuss the previous day's work with the team; plan for the day
09.30–10.00	Discuss the play test results with the designer; plan for the next milestone
10.00–12.00	Program a test prototype of the next task
12.00–1.00 pm	Lunch
1.00–1.30	Show the prototype to the team; get feedback
1.30–5.00	Start programming the real thing
5.00–5.30	Put all the new bits together; everyone plays it before home time
OR	
5.30–???	If a milestone is due, we order pizza and keep working until it's done – sometimes all night!

Note to self

A publisher pays for the game one month at a time, checking that it's OK before paying the next instalment. These are called milestones, and it's important to hit these dates – otherwise you don't get paid!

How I became a game developer

My first home computer was a Sinclair ZX81.

I've always been fascinated with computers and games. My first experience with video games was spending my pocket money playing *Space Invaders* and *Donkey Kong* arcade machines at my local corner shop. I used my powers of persuasion to convince my parents to buy me ever more powerful home computers.

Every upgrade allowed me to write and play more impressive games. Although sold for playing games just like modern gaming consoles, every one of them came with a keyboard and a programming language called Basic. I bought *Zzap!64* magazine each month, and spent hours typing in the demo programs it included.

My first game console was an Atari 2600.

Gaining inspiration

I played classic games such as *Zelda*, *Mario*, and *Sonic*. Home internet access was rare, so I read gaming magazines to find out the names of the developers and sometimes cut out their photos. I realized that these people were sitting down at a keyboard, using a programming language, and making games. If they could do it, then maybe I could too! I was always thinking up crazy ideas for games and sketching out designs for characters.

An expensive hobby

My father was a miner, so the only way I could afford computer games was to save my pocket money, get a paper round, and convince my family to give me money instead of presents at Christmas and birthdays. Luckily, these days even a modestly priced PC is at least 1,000 times more powerful than any of my old home computers, so there's no need to constantly upgrade!

The BBC Micro Model B (1981) had the best version of Basic I'd ever seen.

School

I spent so much time programming that my school work suffered. There were no computer studies or IT classes as there are today. At home, I was learning how to code text adventure games and make small animations. My Engineering Drawing teacher (a class I loved) got me into college studying BTEC engineering, even though my grades weren't great. I wish I'd concentrated more on Maths, English, and Science, because at college I had to take night classes just to catch up!

Did you know?

The Raspberry Pi is a new minicomputer for children costing just $35 (£25). It runs Linux (like Windows, but free) and can connect to a mouse, keyboard, and TV. It can run programming languages such as Python and Scratch. You can save your work to an SD card (like you'd find in a digital camera). It doesn't have a case, but you can make one from Lego!

College

I studied hard and had access to the BBC Micro, a powerful, expensive computer. It was developed by the BBC TV company to encourage young people to program. There was even a TV series about it called *The Computer Programme*.

Making my own games

It was while using the BBC Micro that I first played *Elite*. Released in 1984, it's one of the earliest 3D games. It allowed the player to explore space in their own ship! I was astounded by this game and became determined to understand how it had been made.

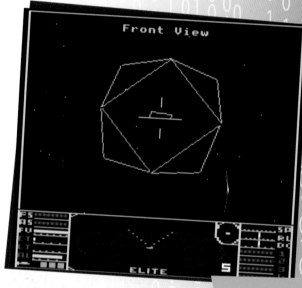

Coding

I learned how to program very small devices in the language Assembler, which doesn't have many commands. These programs run on tiny chips inside everyday appliances such as televisions. While Basic feels similar to English, Assembler feels quite alien as it's closer to the language of the computer, machine code. I worked with chips called the Z80 and the 6502. They were also used in the ZX81, Spectrum, and Game Gear.

I loved trying to dock my ship with a space station in *Elite*.

Did you know?

Games such as *Elite* are too big to be made by people, so the computer uses rules to build it all randomly. It's called procedural generation, and in *Elite* the rules control distances between stars, planet size, how many pirates attack, and so on. Although *Elite* looks simple, it contained eight galaxies, each with 256 planets.

This is a tiny Z80 CPU, which was the heart of many games consoles.

Doing sums in Assembler versus Basic

Let's say we need to do a simple calculation. Which one makes sense to you? In Basic, we'd use one line and it's easier to read than Assembler. In Basic, we can write the programme much faster, but an Assembler version could run 1,000 times faster. Assembler is still used in games, but only in the 1 per cent of the code that needs to be super-fast.

Z80 Assembler

```
LD A, 23
LD B, 100
LD C, 53
ADD A,B
SUB C
```

Register "A" equals 70

Basic

```
result = (100 + 23) − 53
```

Variable "result" equals 70

15

University

My BTEC diploma was just enough to get into university – if I'd studied harder at school then life would've been easier! At university, I studied Information Technology. I learned about networking, programming, and computer systems, and decided programming was what I really loved. This was where I honed my skills with the language C++. It's very common in the games industry.

Hurrah for Sheffield Hallam University! That's where I learned what I needed to know to start my career.

When I finished university, I spent three months creating a demo of spinning 3D shapes and sent this to many game companies. 3D was still fairly new, and I hoped they'd be impressed that I'd managed it alone. A company called Gremlin Interactive hired me, and I've been making games ever since.

C++

A game quickly gets complicated as you write more and more code. Simple languages such as Basic, which are great for novices, soon start to slow down. C++ was designed to be very fast and handle really big programs. I'd expect a C++ program to be 50 to 100 times faster than the equivalent in Basic.

TOOLS OF THE TRADE: SMALL BASIC AND C++

Here are two programs that do the same thing: put 100 enemy units on screen in rows of 10. (Note: the lines in italics are not part of the programs.) It may seem odd, but the longer program actually runs faster. If you want to write something simple quickly, use Small Basic, but if you want it running fast, use C++.

Small Basic

```
'setup 100 enemy positions
'in rows of 10
For index = 0 To 99
    enemies[index]["x"] = Math.GetRandomNumber(800)
    enemies[index]["y"] = Math.Floor(index/10) * 50
EndFor
```

C++

```
//first define what an enemy is
class Enemy
{
public:
    int x,y;
    Sprite image;
    bool alive;

    void Setup(int _x, int _y)
    {
        x = _x;
        y = _y;
        alive= true;
    }
};

//create 100 enemies
Enemy *enemies = new Enemy[100];
//setup enemy positions in rows of 10
int x, y;
for(int index=0; index<100; ++index)
{
    x = rand()%800;
    y = (index/10) * 50;
    enemies[index].Setup(x, y);
}
```

Different roles, different skills

I've worked in every game development role, but my favourite is programmer. A programmer takes the ideas of the designers, the artwork, sound effects and music, and makes the game work. Although there are many programming languages, they are all similar and it's easy to move from one to another. Programmers have to be focused, logical people with good maths skills. They often work alone or in small groups for weeks at a time on tricky problems.

TOOLS OF THE TRADE: MONITORS

Computer programmers often have two monitors: one running the game and the other running the debugger, which checks for bugs. This is so you can see what's happening "under the hood".

Will Wright is the designer behind *SimCity*, *Spore*, and *The Sims* — the top-selling PC game at over 180 million copies.

Designer

Designers come up with the initial idea for a game, and create a "design bible" that the team refer to. The ideas come from playing different video games. Designers often test their ideas on paper, by making little board games, before asking the team to make a prototype. This is a quick, rough version of the idea, just to test if it's any good. Designers build the actual levels as well as writing the scripts. A script contains the text of the story, character dialogue, and the logic that controls what happens.

Designers need to be able to think creatively and understand a little of all the other roles so that they can communicate their vision to the team and ensure their ideas are realistic.

Did you know?

A modern game such as *Street Fighter* can have half a million lines of code.

Artist

Artists create all the images, models, and textures used in a game. They are often the most flamboyant, exciting, and colourful members of the team. Creative and artistically talented, they also need to use quite complex tools. The most common are 3D Studio Max for making 3D models and Photoshop for 2D art and textures.

Did you know?

Artists produce hundreds of different images of surfaces when they build games, whether it's rocks, grass, water, or wood. This means they'll often be sent on location to photograph places or objects to ensure their work is realistic.

This model from *Gunmetal* (a game I worked on) is half wireframe, half textured. The finished 3D object can be viewed from any angle and appear very realistic.

TOOLS OF THE TRADE: SOFTWARE

Instead of an expensive mixing studio, audio engineers often use software instead. A programme such as Reason can simulate mixing desk, synthesizers, effects, and every other piece of expensive hardware, using a single computer and some speakers.

Audio engineer

Part musician and part recording engineer, audio engineers create sound effects and in-game music. Like artists, audio engineers are sent on location. For example, they might visit a race track to make recordings of cars. An audio engineer will usually work with musicians on the soundtrack, and if the game needs an orchestral score or voice actors, then the engineer will supervise the arrangement.

2D images are just normal pictures. They may not look realistic, but can still be beautiful. This is an example from one of my games, Starscape.

Audio engineers need to be talented musicians, expert studio engineers, and have good organizational skills.

Producer

On every game team, there is always a producer whose job it is to make sure that the game gets finished on time, and any problems get fixed fast. Producers keep themselves separate from the team and it can be a lonely job; they're effectively in charge and have to make sure everyone does enough work to meet all the milestones. A producer needs to be a good communicator. They need to be very well organized as they have to keep detailed records about what everyone is doing.

MY HERO!
KELLEE SANTIAGO

Kellee Santiago was the producer and one of the design team of the games *Flow, Flower*, and *Journey*. The games industry needs more female developers like her. Half of all gamers are female, yet 96 per cent of developers are male!

START HERE

GA

ACA
GAME

MY HERO!
SHIGERU MIYAMOTO
(BORN 1952)

Shigeru Miyamoto is one of my all-time heroes. He's probably the most famous games producer and designer in the world. Even if you don't know his name, you'll know his games – this is the man behind *Super Mario*, *Donkey Kong*, and *Zelda*.

Tester

Before a game is released, it must undergo many hours of testing. It would take one person years to complete it all, so games companies use teams of testers. It sounds like the greatest job in the world, playing games all day, but testers have to be very methodical and focused. Good communication skills are essential if they are to clearly explain why some aspect of the game just doesn't "feel" right.

Did you know?

"Bug" is the name given to errors in game code that might make the game crash. All developers must watch out for them!

Game genres

There are many types of games, but most fall into
a surprisingly small number of categories or
genres defining how the game will play.

Role Playing Games

In a Role Playing Game (RPG), the player takes on the lead role in a story and
only by developing that character can the story be completed successfully.
Many RPGs have a medieval setting with knights, goblins, and magic.

Many RPGs use a grey scale image called a "height map" to represent
the world. The height map can be drawn by an artist, made randomly by
computer, or taken from real data such as Google Earth. Dark areas are low
like valleys and white areas are high like mountain tops. These height values
create a 3D map over which image textures are draped to represent grass,
stone, water, and so on.

This height map
(left) shows
mountains and
valleys (right).

Casual

Casual games are often based on simple puzzles, and can last just a few minutes. They are usually cheap to buy and popular on mobile devices or the web. Sometimes they are free, paid for by adverts. Getting a hit game is tricky, as it's hard to say what is needed for people to fall in love with such simple games. For example, *Angry Birds'* developer, Rovio, made 51 other games before they struck gold. *Angry Birds* is massively popular and has been downloaded over 1 billion times.

LOADING...

Did you know?

Angry Birds uses a physics simulation of balls hitting bricks under gravity, so everything crashes down realistically. There are many different physics games, but the simulation is usually the same.

First Person Shooter

First Person Shooter (FPS) focuses on guns, and the player experiences the action through the eyes of the main character. The genre is controversial, due to its obsession with violence. However, research has shown that even very young children know the difference between play and the real thing. One leading FPS has made $6 billion (£3.7 billion) and been played online by over 30 million people.

This is *Gunmetal*. I worked on it's artificial intelligence (AI), and it took weeks to stop the enemies from running in circles and getting stuck.

GoldenEye was released in 1997. I was amazed by how fast and exciting it felt.

Sports games

Sports games are very popular, and are often released each year with only minor alterations, as the members of football teams change or the starting line up in Formula 1 changes, for example. In football games, motion capture is used to accurately represent people moving.

I made a point of "volunteering" when Alan Shearer, former England captain, visited to record his voice-over for Actua Soccer.

People can tell if an artist animates someone moving – it never looks quite right. Instead, special cameras are used to capture the real motion of actors.

Massively Multiplayer Online (MMO)

A massively multiplayer game allows thousands of people to play together at the same time. For example, *World of Warcraft* holds the record for the maximum number of paying subscribers at 12 million, although only about 4,500 play together at any one time on a single server. An MMO needs servers and complex network code written by highly paid specialist game programmers.

EVE
ONLINE

INFERNO

EVE Online is a sci-fi game that holds the world record for numbers of people playing together at once: 63,170 people!

HOPE TOWN

A few of my indie games are MrRobot, Starscape, and Word Pirate. Here is Word Pirate. Small, but perfectly formed!

buy and sell at the market

Wreckers and pirates used the town's well protected harbour, but there was no permanent settlement until the late 1700s. A coastline of rocky bays, tiny inlets and cays made for a great pirate hideout while being close to major shipping lanes

Indie games

Most recently, I've worked with a small team of friends as an indie game developer. We only work on small games that are sold through specialist channels such as Steam, Xbox Live Indie Games, Playstation Network, or that are downloaded directly from the developer's website.

An indie game usually caters to small audiences who want something different like "shootemups", puzzle games, or 2D adventure games. Often, these are genres that were really popular years ago, but now have only 10,000–100,000 fans and are ignored by big publishers.

Note to self

I worked on the prototype for a sci-fi MMO, but the publisher wasn't sure and pulled the plug. I was really upset, but you have to learn to accept it and move on – or become indie and make it yourself!

Physical games

One of the newest genres is aimed at getting people moving. The Nintendo Wii and Sony PS3 both have controllers that the player can wave around to control the action. The Xbox 360 has its Kinect camera that can capture the player's whole body, in a similar way to the motion capture that games designers use.

Some mobile phone games can even use your current location and pictures of real world objects in treasure hunt games, or overlay game content on live camera video. The developer must be careful of over-tiring the player, and they must write code that can detect if the player is performing the correct move or not.

This game is controlled using a Kinect camera.

In a simulation game such as *The Sims*, everything depends on how the player alters the simulation. The game can play out completely differently from one play session to the next.

Simulation games

Simulation games often don't have a story, and you usually can't even control any of the characters directly. Sometimes the games don't even have an end! The game simulates an interesting period in history, an event or situation, and then lets the player alter the simulation and see what happens. These games are very complex programs to write and test, as they don't play out like a normal game with a predefined plot.

One of my favourites is *Civilisation* from 1991, by the wonderful game designer Sid Meier. It allows you to simulate the entire history of Earth! You can play it as a warlike dictator, peaceful diplomat, or anything in between. Games can often be a bit boring once you've played them once, but a good sim game such as *Civilisation* is never the same twice.

Different ways of working

Games are designed for many different platforms. Sometimes you can even play the same game on several different devices. They're all different – some are easy to work on, some hard.

Console

Traditionally, many gamers played on mainstream consoles such as the Nintendo Entertainment System or Xbox. Games for these consoles have a huge potential audience, but developing for them is expensive. You need a contract with Sony, Microsoft, or Nintendo, and a special development version of their console to hook up to your PC.

The Xbox live indie games channel is a great place to find indie games.

Community   Powered   Play

However, Microsoft and Sony are willing to work with indie developers, and that can be far cheaper. It sounds great, but they are probably not doing this just out of the kindness of their hearts. Working with indie developers is a great way to get even more great games, for free, which help sell their consoles. It's a tough way into the market – fewer than 1 per cent of developers strike it rich in this way.

PCs

Many people play games on PCs as well. The PC, whether Windows, Macintosh, or Linux based, allows open development. This means anyone can make any game they like, put it online, sell it, and keep all the money. However, the Steam app store is where most people buy their games, so it's not quite as free as it initially seems.

MY HERO!
JOHN CARMACK
(BORN 1970)

John Carmack is one of my heroes. He was the programming genius behind *Wolfenstein 3D*, a groundbreaking game for the PC platform. He was constantly developing or popularizing new techniques in computer graphics.

John Carmack

Mobile

One of the fastest growing types of games is "apps" for mobile devices such as smartphone and tablets. Two of the main platforms involved are iPhone and Android. Games for these platforms are fairly simple to make and sell online, so many people are trying to strike it rich this way.

Most mobile developers use software libraries to help them get their games working. For example, Marmalade has thousands of lines of code written by experts. Just like a real library, you can pick and choose what you want.

Mobile games are often ten times cheaper than console games, and are sometimes even free.

Web

There are thousands of free games playable through websites and they are written in Flash, Unity, Java, or HTML5. The developer's income usually comes from one of the large gaming websites. These websites are always looking for new games. The games are usually small and simple, so don't take long to make (6–12 weeks usually).

Electronic Arts is one of the world's largest game publishers, with over 9,000 staff.

Game developers

There are different types of game developer working in different genres. The main difference between them is the size of the budget, which limits the number of staff. Big publishers such as Microsoft, Sony, Electronic Arts, Sega, and Nintendo employ thousands of developers. They can work in huge teams of up to 200 people on blockbuster games such as *The Sims*, which make billions of dollars.

Did you know?

Sometimes a game crashes, meaning that it just stops working. This is usually caused by a bug. It's essential that all crash bugs are fixed before the game is released.

250 SHORELINE DRIVE

EA ELECTRONIC ARTS

Work for hire

There are thousands of small companies, employing 15–100 developers, who work for any publisher that needs them. A work-for-hire developer sends its producers to visit publishers each time it needs a new project. They usually have a specific idea or character they need making into a smaller game: for example *Sonic* or *Wario*.

Did you know?

Developers can't stop adding new ideas – this is called feature creep. But once we hit Alpha, the producer has to put a stop to it. Every feature added makes the game a little more complex and a little harder to test.

TOOLS OF THE TRADE: HOME COMFORTS

When I worked at Rage Games, I had a sleeping bag ready for if I got tired while working late. I also had my own mini fridge, posters, and my desk was decorated with collectable game and film figures.

Sumo made *Sonic & Sega All Stars Racing* and the *Dr. Who* adventure games.

Indie companies

An indie game company will consist of 1–15 developers, usually without the support of a publisher. They will come together to work on something new, and if they are talented and lucky, they'll get a mega-hit that makes millions. However, because they are working on something completely new, it might not make any money at all. I love running an indie game company: we get total freedom to explore all our crazy game ideas. There's more to life than making money!

Indies have to be very creative to come up with completely new ideas.

Learning to make games

Many games allow players to make their own levels. Making your own level in something like *Little Big Planet* and then sharing it with other players online is a fantastic experience for a budding designer.

Sometimes, lots of players come together to make something that feels almost completely different from the original game. This requires amateur artists, programmers, designers, and musicians to get together over the internet. If it's popular enough, the company might even hire them. This happened with *Portal*.

MY FAVOURITE GAME

Everyone should play *Portal 1* and *Portal 2*. I love them and think they are absolutely fantastic examples of gaming at its best. *Portal's* editor is even used in some schools to teach physics!

Prototyping

You can learn a lot by playing and making board games or card games. The fastest way to test a new game idea is to make a board game or card game version of it, and this happens at a lot of game studios. When playing a video game it can be hard to work out how the developer actually made it work, but when you play a card game or board game the rules are laid out in detail. Most game developers I know play table top games. I particularly enjoy *Magic*, *The Gathering*, *Talisman*, *Arkham Horror*, and *Mansions of Madness*.

MY FAVOURITE GAME

Arkham Horror is my favourite board game. It takes hours to play and is very complicated, but the rules are beautiful and link together like clockwork to make the closest thing to a video game on your table top.

What goes into a video game?

I'm going to take a game I made called *Starscape* and split it apart into all the different sections that needed implementing. This is like a film storyboard, and it helps the team visualize how all the different parts of the game fit together.

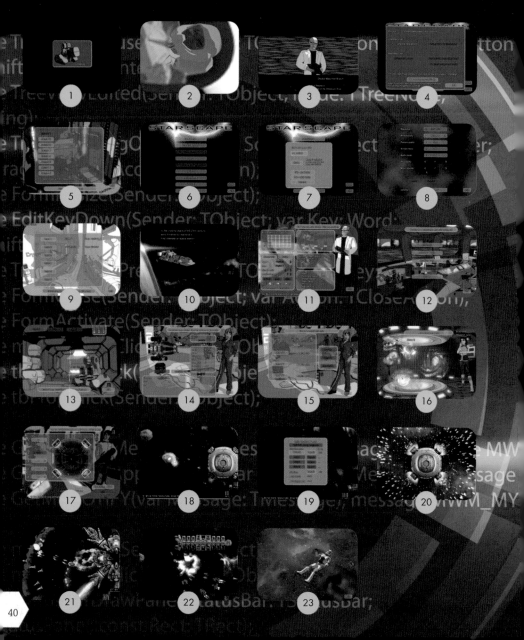

Key

1. Pre-load: it will take about 10 seconds to load the game.
2. Splash: show the Moonpod animation – this is the same on all my games.
3. General introduction: introduce the characters and overall story.
4. Unlock: after downloading from a website, players need a way to pay for the game.
5. Hall of fame: the top ten players' names and scores.
6. Main menu: from here we can access options, new game, load, save, etc.
7. New game: type in your name and set the difficulty you want.
8. Options: set the screen resolution, volume level, etc.
9. Save and load: save a game or load an old one.
10. Main intro: show a detailed animation introducing your part in the story.
11. Research: decide what equipment you'd like to work on next.
12. In game menu: choose which part of the game to visit from here.
13. Storage: review all the equipment you've made or found, but aren't using.
14. Ship modification: change the equipment attached to a ship.
15. Docking bays: select which ship to modify.
16. Navigation: use the maps to navigate around space.
17. Modify station: attach equipment to your space station.
18. Space: fly, fight, mine, shoot asteroids, collect items, and talk to people.
19. Station options: launch a fighter or warp out of the level.
20. Warp: warp in and out of levels.
21. Boss fight: levels are grouped into areas; each area has a big boss to fight.
22. Death: when you die, go out with a bang!
23. Death animation: mark your passing and display a summary of achievements.

Quiz

Interested in working in the games industry, but not sure
what role you're best suited for? Try this fun quiz to see
which job best suits your personality and skills.

1. **It's time to go on holiday! However, your spending money is fixed, so
    you can't afford to visit all the attractions. What should you do?**

    a) Let's get all the facts and figures into a spreadsheet.

    b) I don't care if I run out of money – I just want to take photos and gaze
    at the sunsets.

    c) Jonny's good at this kind of thing; she went there last year, so let's
    get her to help.

    d) If I write everything down carefully, I can try different combinations.

    e) If I run out of money, I'll just make up my own entertainment – it's
    no biggie.

    f) I just want to talk to everyone, really get to know the place, and visit
    the cafés with the best music.

2. **The school magazine is interviewing you. What do you think about school?**

    a) I like Maths, Science, and Computer Studies best. Last week, I built a
    water-powered rocket that really worked.

    b) I like art and design lessons, and I love showing my friends what
    I've made.

    c) I like working on group projects and socializing, but sometimes people
    say I'm bossy.

    d) I like coursework. I spend a lot of time making sure my work is neat
    and well laid out.

    e) I don't really like being told what to do or doing anything boring. I like
    it when we can pick our own projects to work on.

    f) I like Computer Studies, foreign languages, and music lessons best.

3. **What are your hobbies? Let's assume playing games is number one!**

    a) I like taking things apart to see how they work, and building models.

    b) I like going to art galleries, cutting out pictures from magazines for
    scrap books, and craft projects.

c) I've joined lots of clubs and I like being with my gang of friends.

d) I like making lists and keeping all my collections properly organized.

e) I don't mind being on my own; I read a lot, sometimes write stories, and enjoy walks in the countryside where I can think clearly. I play board games with friends.

f) I'm learning to play an instrument, and I've uploaded some tracks I made to the internet.

4. The school is putting on a show. How will you get involved?

a) I think it's time for some impressive special effects and a pre-designed light show.

b) I'd love to do the stage dressing or the costumes.

c) I'll have to direct: I already know who'll make a great lead.

d) I could help everyone with their lines and prompt anyone who fluffs one.

e) I think we should do our own play for once. In fact, I've got some great ideas for a show.

f) It's got to be a musical, and I'm sure a live orchestra would be better than the usual prerecording.

Answers

Mainly A: You are a logical person who would make a great programmer.

Mainly B: You are creative and artistic, so consider a career as a game artist.

Mainly C: You like to take charge and organize people, so a producer would be a good choice.

Mainly D: You are methodical and careful, so you'd make a good games tester.

Mainly E: You have a powerful imagination and are full of ideas, which is perfect for a designer.

Mainly F: You have a good ear, so consider becoming an audio engineer.

Glossary

Alpha point in a game's development when all the tools are finished and it's time to build the levels

artificial intelligence (AI) code that makes the computer opponent seem realistic, like you're playing against a person

Assembler complicated low level programming language used when super speed is needed

Basic simple programming language designed for novice programmers

beta point in a game's development when it's finished but contains a lot of bugs that need fixing

bug error in a computer program

C++ powerful, but complex language used to produce nearly all console and PC games. C++ is often a requirement for a game programming job.

certification a publisher uses its own testers to certify a new game works properly on a particular console, like the Xbox 360 or PS3

CPU central processing unit. This is the silicon chip at the heart of a computer, games console, tablet, or phone. It used to be accompanied by many other chips that handled sound, graphics, and so on, but it's more common today to find one large chip that does everything.

debugger special software that lets you monitor a game as it runs and helps track down bugs that make the game crash

demo demonstration

games console early examples came with Basic, but now they no longer have keyboards and are dedicated to playing games only

genre style or category of game, such as role-player game or casual game

home computer although it can be used to play games, it can also be used for many other tasks, even making games

milestone usually a monthly check on the progress of a game's development; if the game doesn't pass then the publisher may withhold payments to the programmer or company

motion capture special cameras that capture the movement of actors and allow computers to replay that movement to create realistic animation

physics rules describing how objects move, fall, and collide

platform hardware or environment that a game must run on. A PC windows platform is different from a tablet Android platform, and this needs to be dealt with in the computer code.

producer person responsible for ensuring a game is finished on time

prototype quick, rough version of an idea used to test if it's any good

prototyping trying to very quickly test how a small part of a game might look or play. It's a way of experimenting without spending a year making the whole game.

Python popular programming language sometimes used by professionals for game scripting

random code that changes things every time it runs, ensuring a game doesn't play the same every go

server computer that hosts games, usually on the internet, so people can play together

simulation recreation of a real thing

texture picture used to wrap around a 3D game object to make it look solid, for example a photo of a footballer's face wrapped around his in-game model's head

variable in programs we often need to hang on to numbers or text and we can store this data temporarily in a named variable. It's like getting a box, putting important things in it, and then sticking on a label so that you can find it again later.

wireframe if you take the textures off a 3D game object, you're left with just the scaffolding or wires defining the shape

Find out more

Books

Computer Game and Film Graphics (Art Off the Wall), Paul Byrne
(Heinemann Library, 2007)

Super Scratch Programming Adventure!: Learn to Program by Making Cool Games,
The LEAD Project (No Starch Press, 2012)

Video Game Programming for Kids, Jonathan S. Harbour (Delmar Cengage
Learning, 2012)

Websites

www.appinventor.mit.edu

Want to make mobile games, but C++ is too tricky? App Inventor is a bit like Scratch
and is very easy to use – you just snap together bits of code, and it's free!

gaming.adobe.com/getstarted

Want to make a web game using Flash? If you're at school, you can get a copy of the
software you need for free.

www.kodugamelab.com

Kodu is also for those new to programming; it's free and made by Microsoft. For a small
fee, you can also get a version that works on an Xbox 360. Unlike Scratch, you can
actually make 3D games.

www.ludumdare.com/compo

Want to try out your new skills and meet other programmers? Ludumdare is a regular
online competition and forum that gives you a theme and lets you make a game around
that theme in 48 hours.

www.madewithmarmalade.com

If you've got your C++ mojo working, but want to make games for mobile phones and tablets, get a free copy of Marmalade to take care of the boring bits.

www.microsoft.com/visualstudio/en-us/products/2010-editions/visual-cpp-express

Games on consoles are written in C++. Visual Studio is one of the most common packages used in the industry and this "express" version is free!

www.moonpod.com

This is my indie gaming website. You can play some of the games I made for free, ask a question on the forum, or just say hello.

www.pygame.org/news.html

This simple-to-use programming language is free, and is a good option to try after Small Basic.

scratch.mit.edu

If you're new to programming, this is the place to start. Scratch is free and easy to learn. Have a look at my page: scratch.mit.edu/projects/MarkFeatherstone/2503601.

smallbasic.com

Try Microsoft's free version of Basic after you've mastered Scratch or Kodu. It can also be an introduction to Visual Basic, which could help to get you a job in the future.

Topic for research

Ask your Computer Studies teacher if you can organize a game competition, maybe using Scratch, and get everyone in your class involved.

Index